THE COMPLETE
HEALTHY
SMOOTHIE
FOR NUTRIBULLET

Skyhorse Publishing books may be purchased in bulk at special discounts for sales promotion, corporate gifts, fund-raising, or educational purposes. Special editions can also be created to specifications. For details, contact the Special Sales Department, Skyhorse Publishing, 307 West 36th Street, 11th Floor, New York, NY 10018 or info@ skyhorsepublishing.com.

Skyhorse® and Skyhorse Publishing® are registered trademarks of Skyhorse Publishing, Inc.®, a Delaware corporation.

Visit our website at www.skyhorsepublishing.com.

10 9 8 7 6 5 4 3 2 1

Library of Congress Cataloging-in-Publication Data is available on file.

Cover design by Brian Peterson
Cover photo credit: Leo Quijano II

Print ISBN: 978-1-63450-871-1
Ebook ISBN: 978-1-63450-701-1

Printed in China

THE COMPLETE
HEALTHY
SMOOTHIE
FOR NUTRIBULLET

JASON MANHEIM

Skyhorse Publishing, Inc.

CONTENTS

The Complete HEALTHY **Smoothie** for NUTRIBULLET

Introduction

We look to healthy smoothies in order to assure ourselves that even when time is fleeting, we are still able to get in at least one meal or snack that is both satiating and nutritious. Wouldn't it be nice if convenience, cost and time efficiency, and ease of use—all attributes that can be associated with smoothies—were also attributes we could apply to the mechanisms and ingredients needed to create that smoothie? High-powered blenders are nice, if you can afford them but for our purposes, they are entirely superfluous.

Truth be told, a year ago I would have insisted that a top of the line blender was a requirement if you were serious about your healthy smoothie routine. Today, I'm singing a different tune. It has been nearly nine months since I've even plugged in my expensive blender. Why? *The NutriBullet.*

I am already convinced that a healthy green smoothie in the morning is the perfect way to give my body the nutrition it needs in a way that is incredibly quick and easy. I simply overlooked the NutriBullet because I could not imagine the process becoming any more streamlined. Boy was I wrong. I can wake up, make a smoothie, and be in my office, sipping away and beginning work in less than two minutes. *Two minutes!* The convenience of having the blending container be the same cup I drink from all but eliminates cleanup, limits the serving size, and even allows me to premix my ingredient ahead of time so they're ready to toss on the motor, blend, and get on with my day.

As of this writing, the NutriBullet comes in three varieties:

- Original for $90 (600 watts)
- Pro for $130 (900 watts)
- RX for $200 (1700 watts)

All recipes in this book have been tested with the Original NutriBullet (600 watts) using the 24-ounce cup. This is usually one serving. However, feel free to drink half, cap it, refrigerate, and drink the remaining half within 24 hours for minimal nutrient loss.

A few things to keep in mind that are specific the NutriBullet:

- Some people will have a difficult time getting past the gritty elements of harder/waxier skins and leaves which the NutriBullet may have a hard time blending to a smooth texture. In the case of apples, you may skin them. Keep in mind however, the skins of apples contain a great deal of nutritional content so I'd urge you to experiment with blending longer or adding more liquid if texture is an issue. For leaves like kale and collard greens you can use baby varieties which are softer and less waxy, or substitute with something like spinach.

- Add all solid ingredients before liquid and ice. You will need to experiment a bit with the amount of water/liquid/ice used for each recipe. A good rule of thumb is to fill the NutriBullet container at least halfway with liquid. I typically top it off with a handful of ice cubes.

- You can purchase extra blending cups for $10. Consider buying a few to make your routine even easier by picking a day, say Sundays, and prefill a bunch of cups for the week. That way you can toss one on the motor and blend whenever you're feeling pressed for time and need a meal. It helps a lot with avoiding foods that are less nutritious as well.

The following 100+ recipes are all that you need to enjoy a variety of healthy smoothies all year long.

1. A Grape Pear

Ingredients

1 handful green grapes
½ pear
1 handful baby kale
½ orange (peeled)
½ banana (optional)
water/ice

Fill NutriBullet with as much water/ice as you like and add kale. Blend until smooth. Add fruit. Blend until desired consistency.

A grape . . . I mean, great one for the novice green drinker. The pear, grapes, orange and banana make for a sweet enough smoothie while still providing the nutritional benefits from the kale.

2. What-A-Lemon

Ingredients

2 cups watermelon
1 small bunch watercress
½ roma tomato
½ lemon (juiced)
1 tbsp. olive oil
water/ice

Blend with ice to desired consistency.

3. Apple Raz

Ingredients

½ red apple
1 cup fresh raspberries
⅛ honeydew melon
1 small handful baby kale
1 small handful baby
  greens
1 lemon (juice)
½ banana (optional)
water/ice

Fill Nutribullet with water/ice, add kale, greens, and apple. Blend until smooth. Add remaining ingredients. Blend until desired consistency.

The sweetness of the red apple and the sour tang of the fresh raspberries and lemon balance out the bold flavor of the calcium rich kale. Baby greens add a boost of vitamins and really makes this a well-rounded green drink.

A great way to kick off your morning!

4. Apple Sprouts

Ingredients

⅛ small red onion
½ apple
½ pear
1 handful spinach
2–3 brussels sprouts
   (cooked 3–4 minutes)
ginger to taste
water/ice

Blend with water and ice
to desired consistency.

5. The Healthy Green Drink

Ingredients

1 small bunch watercress
½ green apple
½ lime (peeled)
¼ English cucumber
4 mint leaves
½ banana (optional)
water/ice

Fill NutriBullet with as much water/ice as you like and add ingredients. Blend until smooth.

As the title track in our album of health, The Healthy Green Drink is a powerhouse of nutrition and taste.

Watercress, which can be commonly found at local Farmer's Markets and grocery stores, is often overlooked. It adds a wonderful spiciness while the mint, cucumber combination cools it down. A refreshing accompaniment to any meal.

6. Sangria Blanca

Ingredients

½ white peaches (pitted)
½ cup rainier cherries
   (pitted)
½ white nectarines
   (pitted)
½ cup green grapes
3–6 endive leaves
2–4 mint leaves
water/ice

Blend with water and ice
to desired consistency.

7. Just Peachy

Ingredients

1–2 whole peaches (pitted)
1 cups spinach
water/ice

Fill NutriBullet with as much water/ice as you like and add ingredients. Blend until smooth.

Here's a simple one. *Great for kids and those having trouble incorporating greens into their diets.*

Spinach really packs a punch. It's a common green, you can get it just about anywhere, it's affordable and the taste is mild enough that anyone can enjoy it. It's a great source of iron and beta-carotene and protects from a multitude of maladies. And who doesn't like peaches?

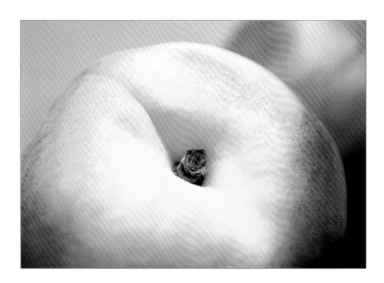

8. Mangomole

Ingredients

½ cup mango
½ peach
1 handful spinach
1 small bunch cilantro
⅛ small onion
⅛ avocado
¼ yellow bell pepper
jalapeno to taste
½ lemon (juiced)
water/ice

Blend with water and ice to desired consistency.

9. Beauty Berry

Ingredients

½ of a ripe avocado
1 tablespoon soaked goji berries
1 tablespoon raw honey
½ cup whole milk yogurt
½ small cucumber
1 cup coconut water

Blend all ingredients together and serve with a straw.

This drink couldn't be better for you if you wore it on your face. These high antioxidant free-radical fighters combine to give you and your skin a healthy glow. This one can make you beautiful on the inside as well as the outside.

Change it up: *Reduce coconut water to ½ cup and blend to make a delectable face mask that combats dry skin. Apply with fingers, careful not to get too close to your eyes. This is a wet mask, so leave it on for about 25 minutes before rinsing off with warm water.*

10. Mango Mint-jito

Ingredients

½ cup mango
1 cup lettuce greens
4 large mint leaves
½ lemon (juice)
½ lime (juice)
½ banana (optional)
water/ice

Fill NutriBullet with as much water/ice as you like, adding mint and greens. Blend until smooth. Add fruit. Blend until desired consistency.

For the lush in all of us. Except, you know . . . without all the stumbling and liver damage. If fact, with the amount of fiber and enzymes in mangoes, you can lower LDL cholesterol and improve digestion.

A fresher, healthier approach to its boozier counterpart, the Mango Mint-jitos sweet tropical flavors will leave you hungry for a day by the pool instead of a night hugging the toilet.

11. Gazpatcho

Ingredients

1 Roma tomato
¼ red bell pepper
1 small garlic clove
⅛ small onion
1 small handful cilantro
1 small handful parsley
jalapeno to taste
tarragon to taste
water/ice

Blend with water and ice
to desired consistency.

12. Strawberry Patch

Ingredients

3 strawberries
½ mango
½ kiwi
2–3 big basil leaves
1 large collard leaf
(remove stem)
water

Fill NutriBullet with as much water as you like, adding collard greens and basil. Blend until smooth. Add fruit. Blend until desired consistency.

A sweet treat and an easy way to introduce dark greens like collards into your diet. Collards have a strong, distinct flavor especially when cooked, but when blended raw among earthy-sweet and tropical flavors like kiwi and strawberry you'll find collards are great at adding a spicy zing to an otherwise typical fruit smoothie.

Mangoes add a list of health benefits to the smoothie with enzymes that aid healthy digestion, glutamine for memory power and heart-healthy antioxidants.

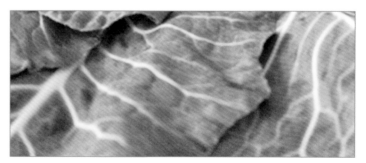

13. Cosmo Chiller

Ingredients

1 cup mustard greens
¼ medium cucumber
½ cup frozen cranberries
½ lime (juiced)
½ lemon (juiced)
2–4 mint leaves
water/ice

Blend with water and ice to desired consistency.

14. Straw-megranate

Ingredients

3–4 strawberries
½ cup pomegranate juice
¼ red apple
½ stalk celery (soft/white)
½ peach
1 small handful red grapes
1–2 handfuls fresh spinach
½ banana (optional)
water

Fill NutriBullet with as much water as you like. And ingredients. Blend until smooth.

Big, bold strawberry flavor with a tarty pomegranate kick. This antioxidant rich smoothie may decrease the risk of heart disease and guard against free radical damage.

15. Golden Pear

Ingredients

½–1 pear
1 cup cantaloupe
⅛ yellow bell pepper
⅛ small red onion
¼ cup mustard greens
   (cooked 1–2 minutes)
2–3 cabbage leaves
   (cooked 1–2 minutes)
water/ice

Blend with water and ice
to desired consistency.

16. Black Melon

Ingredients

½ cup watermelon
¼ cup honeydew melon
¼ cup cantaloupe
½ cup blackberries
2 handfuls fresh spinach
½ banana (optional)
water/ice

Fill NutriBullet with as much water/ice as you like, adding greens. Blend until smooth. Add fruit. Blend until desired consistency.

An easy way to start introducing greens into your smoothies is to start off sweet. This drink is higher in natural sugars, but still provides essential nutrients without the added preservatives, and refined sugars. Black Melon contains high amounts of antioxidants, fiber, and Vitamin C.

Spinach, an amazing source of protein, has a very subtle flavor and is often completely masked by any sweetness from fruit. Taking care of your body has never tasted so good.

17. Tropicana

Ingredients

1 small handful arugula
½ orange
¼ yellow bell pepper
1 cup pineapple
1 small handful spinach
water/ice

Blend with water and ice
to desired consistency.

18. Green Java

Ingredients

1 cup wheatgrass juice (or
    small bunch watercress)
1 orange (peeled)
½–1 banana (optional)
water/ice

Fill NutriBullet with as
much water/ice as you
like, adding wheatgrass
(if you don't have a high-
powered blender, juice
the wheatgrass first).
Blend until smooth. Add
fruit. Blend until desired
consistency.

*Some of us can't even function until we get our
morning coffee. A quick jolt of caffeine and
energy is all you need, but what you tend to get
is high calories, excess sugar and a tainted smile.
Hardly appealing when you can get twice the
energy boost with none of those downfalls in a
glass of wheatgrass heavy Green Java.*

*Blend juiced wheatgrass with orange and banana
to cut the bite of wheatgrass's intense flavor and
pump you full of Vitamin C and potassium.*

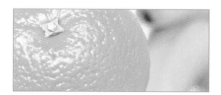

19. Tup-Aloe Honey

Ingredients

1 cup honeydew melon
1 aloe leaves (peeled,
    or ¼ cup juice)
½ kiwi
1 small bunch parsley
1 handful mixed greens
water/ice

Blend with water and ice to desired consistency.

20. Hemp Powered Protein

Ingredients

2 tbsp Hemp seed
1½ tbsp Cacao nibs
¾ cup frozen raspberries
½ cup Whole milk yogurt
¼ tsp Turmeric
1 tbsp Chocolate protein powder
1 cup Coconut water

Place all ingredients in NutriBullet and blend until smooth.

Not your average protein drink, this sinful solution provides the tastiest recovery from a work out you've had that doesn't involve a cheat day. Fruity chocolate raspberry flavor blended with creamy coconut milk and yogurt with a savory hint of turmeric inspires you to skip that cheat day and keep reaching for your goal.

21. Aloeberry

Ingredients

1 large spears fresh aloe
   vera (or ¼ cup bottled)
1 cup spinach
1 large leaf chard
½ green apple
½ cup frozen blueberries
½ banana (optional)

Fill NutriBullet with as much water/ice as you like, adding first 4 ingredients. Blend until smooth. Add fruit. Blend until desired consistency.

If you're looking to get more vitamin B12 in your diet without significant meat in take, aloe vera is one of the only suppliers of Vitamin B12 that doesn't come from animal products.

Chard is also a great source of omega-3 fatty acids if you're not the biggest fan of fish or eggs. Aloeberry has a little bit of everything for the vegans out there looking to avoid vitamin deficiency while still delivering an all around great taste and healthful experience.

22. Simply Sweet

Ingredients

1–3 kale leaves (stemmed)
2–3 strawberries
1 banana
water/ice

Blend with water and ice to desired consistency.

Optional Protein: Whey protein powder

23. Tropical Sun

Ingredients

1 small bulb bok choy
½ orange (peeled)
1 cup coconut water
½ cup pineapple
½ banana

Add first 3 ingredients. Blend until smooth. Add fruit. Blend until desired consistency.

You may not be able to make it to the tropics before breakfast, but you can sure make it to the blender to make yourself this delicious flavor get-a-way.

Before your daily grind starts treat yourself to the rich vitamins orange and pineapple have to offer. Bok Choy, categorized as a negative calorie food by it's ability to facilitate the burning of calories, tastes amazing alongside its tropical components. Throw in a tiny umbrella for good measure and you won't be missing any nutrients, all you'll be missing is the beach.

24. Sweet Mint

Ingredients

1 large collard leaf
½ pear
½ kiwi
½ cup blackberries
½ cup blueberries
2–4 mint leaves
water/ice

Blend with water and ice
to desired consistency.

Optional Protein: Chia
seeds

25. Anti-toxi-mint

Ingredients

4 mint leaves
¼ English cucumber
1 large leaf collard greens
   (stemmed)
½ cup frozen acai berries
½ kiwi (peeled)
½ lemon (juiced)

Add first 3 ingredients. Blend until smooth. Add fruit. Blend until desired consistency.

Perfect for you trend dieters out there looking for better skin, anti-aging properties, cancer fighters, and improving cognitive brain function. Truth be told, all greens can deliver these same benefits, but that's just not what the beauty magazines are about these days.

Even still, you can't beat the tart and tangy taste the Anti-toximint delivers while still being the tabloid starlet who can do anything and everything (even help prevent cancer) and taste good doing it.

26. Figgy Cookie

Ingredients

1 bunch red leaf lettuce
¼ cup fennel
½ cup sweet potato
   (pre-cooked)
1–2 figs
1 tbsp. almond butter
1 cup coconut water
1–2 tbsp. vanilla yogurt (optional)
nutmeg to taste
ice

Blend with ice to desired consistency.

27. Green Glow

Ingredients

1 cup mint
2 bunches spinach
1 cup frozen/fresh pineapple
1 Apple–quartered
Ice

Blend all ingredients together and enjoy!

Simple and delicious, Green Glow, will have you glowing too! This no-fuss recipe is a must for beginners who aren't as seasoned with the experimental flavors of green drinks. I personally believe its easy prep and cleanup make it taste even better.

28. Sweet Potato Pie

Ingredients

½ cup semi cooked sweet
    potato
1 tbsp. ground flax
¼ fennel/anise bulb
½ orange (peeled)
1 cup spinach
1 fresh fig
1 cup coconut water
cinnamon to taste

Add all ingredients. Blend
until smooth, adding water
as necessary.

Even if Autumn is not quite yet in the air you can
bring the nostalgia and flavors of the season into
your morning smoothies or have it as dessert.
Sweet potatoes are a nutritional superstar
that are high in dietary fibers, beta-carotene
and complex carbohydrates and are known to
improve blood-sugar regulation and digestion.

Fennel, while adding a warm licorice flavor is
also good for digestive health and often used
to combat bad breath. Ground flaxseed is rich
in omega-3 fatty acids, high in fiber, and adds
a nutty element all together giving you a tasty,
low starch, guilt free take on a classic seasonal
dessert.

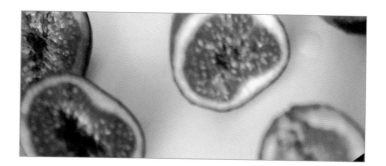

29. Delectable Hulk

Ingredients

1 large handful spinach
1 kiwi
1–3 large basil leaves
½ banana
water/ice

Blend with water and ice
to desired consistency.

30. Just Beet It

Ingredients

1 medium beet (cooked)
1 cup arugula
½ red apple
3 leaves basil
½ banana
water/ice

Add all ingredients. Blend until smooth, adding water as necessary.

Dance around your kitchen threatening unnecessary coffee cakes and pantry snacks to take a hike now that you're on the road to a healthier you. Or you can let your actions speak louder than words and blend up a glass of Just Beet It.

Beets are essential for heart-health and have an earthy-sweet taste. Arugula contains anti-viral and anti-bacterial properties as well as high levels of vitamin K. Though it's known to have a bitter taste, when paired with an apple and banana, there's nothing bitter . . . or should I say, better.

31. Mangorita

Ingredients

½ cup mango
½ orange
1 small handful spinach
½ small handful parsley
½ small handful cilantro
jalapeno to taste
water/ice

Blend with water and ice
to desired consistency.

32. Dumpkin Pie

Ingredients

2 tbsp. pumpkin (either
 fresh or canned)
2 tbsp. raw almond butter
1–2 cups spinach
½ cup frozen blueberries
½ banana
cinnamon or nutmeg to
 taste
water/ice

Add all ingredients. Blend
until smooth, adding water
as necessary.

*This is it, folks, my go-to green smoothie. I can
be a bit vain so I add as much skin-regenerative
pumpkin as I can stomach. The raw almond
butter adds a dose of healthy fats and the
spinach and blueberries give me all the protein,
vitamins and antioxidants I need.*

*Cinnamon turns this strange concoction into
something deliciously pie-latable rather than a
patch of discarded pumpkins decomposing at
the local dump. It's Dumpkin Pie!*

33. Piña Kale-ada

Ingredients

1 cup pineapple
¼ orange
1 leaf rainbow chard
1 kale leaf (stemmed)
½ banana
½ cup coconut milk
water/ice

Blend with ice to desired consistency.

Optional Protein: Whey protein powder

34. Crazy Cran

Ingredients

¼ cup frozen cranberries

¼ orange (peeled)

1 leaf collard greens (stemmed)

1 small bunch mixed baby greens

2–4 mint leaves

¼ pear

1 cup coconut water

½ lemon (juiced)

½ banana (optional)

Add first 4 ingredients. Blend until smooth, adding water, lemon juice, and coconut water as necessary. Add fruit. Pulse-blend until desired consistency.

This is not your regular cranberry cocktail, no sir. This veritable dynamo of vitamins has it all. A high source of fiber in both mixed baby greens and collard greens with mint offering healthful digestive properties, and cranberries providing bacteria blockers.

No jug of juice offers even a fraction of what Crazy Cran brings to the breakfast table. So blend up a glass and toast to your health.

35. Beauty Booster

Ingredients

1 small handful spinach
¼ cup turnip greens
1 tbsp. pureed pumpkin
1–3 dates (pitted)
1 tbsp. flax seed (or oil)
1 cup coconut milk
honey to taste (optional)
water/ice

Blend with water and ice
to desired consistency.

36. Mintal Melon

Ingredients

2–4 leaves mint
1 cup Chinese broccoli
  (cooked for 2–4 minutes)
¼ cup honeydew melon
¼ small cucumber
¼ cup cantaloupe
1 lime (juiced)

Add first 2 ingredients.
Blend until smooth,
adding water and lime
juice as necessary. Add
fruit. Blend until desired
consistency.

Clear your mind with this refreshing Summer drink. Mint will sooth that upset stomach, put an end to that ragging headache and release a pleasant aroma that can calm even the craziest folks.

All the while, the broccoli is silently engaged in a fight to the death with that extra cancer inducing sunshine you're getting. You'd be mental not to give this one a try.

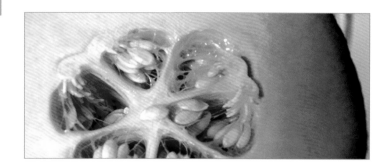

37. Rockin' Berry

Ingredients

1 small handful arugula
½ cup grapes
½ cup blueberries
½ lime (juiced)
2–3 mint leaves
water/ice

Blend with water and ice to desired consistency.

38. Carri-bean cooler

Ingredients

2 carrots - juiced
1 cup frozen/fresh pineapple
2 bunches spinach
1 cup packed mint leaves
1 cup packed basil leaves
¼ jalapeno
Ice

Add ice and blend all ingredients. Top with chia seeds, enjoy, and never go back. Bottoms up.

One glass of this and you'd think you'd gone to heaven, if heaven were somewhere in the tropics where all the drinks are green and health is abundant. You wouldn't be entirely wrong. The sweet heat of this super drink will change the way you think of green drinks. Here's to the beginning of a healthier lifestyle.

39. Liquidate

Ingredients

1 cup lambsquarters
   or dandelion greens
   (cooked 2–3 minutes)
2 dates (pitted)
2 tbsp. raw almond butter
1 cup coconut water
¾ cup frozen blueberries

Add first 2 ingredients. Blend until smooth, adding water and coconut water as necessary. Add fruit and almond butter. Blend until desired consistency.

You're going to hate when this one is gone. Despite the bitter dandelion greens, the dates do an awesome job at turning that bitter to sweet bliss. You'll be purifying your liver and you won't even know it. There's even healthy fats, too.

Replace the blueberries with raspberries and you'll have sweet, bitter and sour all in one.

40. Old Fashioned

Ingredients

1 cup collards
¼ grapefruit
¼ orange
1 tbsp. honey
cayenne pepper to taste
water/ice

Blend with water and ice
to desired consistency.

41. Guavacado

Ingredients

½ cup guava
⅛ avocado
1 cup red leaf lettuce
½ cup mango
½ lemon (juice)
1 cup coconut water

Add all ingredients. Blend until smooth, adding water as necessary.

Guavas can be hard to come by and vary quite drastically in size, shape and texture. Test the seeds before you toss this one into your NutriBullet as some can be as hard as stones.

Also, some guava skin can be thick and bitter so be sure to test that too. All this work just for a smoothie? You won't be disappointed once that creamy avocado texture hits your lips.

42. Georgia Peach

Ingredients

1 handful spinach
½ cup collards
1 small peach (pitted)
½ apple
ginger to taste
water/ice

Blend with water and ice
to desired consistency.

43. Heavy Green

Ingredients

½ cup broccoli (cooked
  3–4 minutes)
1 leaf collard greens
  (stemmed)
½ cup spinach
½ green apple
⅛ cucumber
⅛ avocado
1 lime (juiced)
water

Add all ingredients. Blend
until smooth, adding water
as necessary.

*Green drink newbies need not apply, this one
is for the hardcore green enthusiast. With
minimal amounts of fructose, those with blood
sugar issues will rejoice at this offering. Spinach,
broccoli AND collards!*

*Top it of with the superfood, avocado and you'll
be brimming with a cancer-fighting, nutrient
dense glow. A savory treat not to be missed.*

44. Chili Down

Ingredients

1 small bunch dandelion
   greens
1 Roma tomato
¾ lemon (juiced)
1 tbsp. olive oil
chili powder to taste
water/ice

Blend with water and ice
to desired consistency.

45. Hit Pearade

Ingredients

½ cup radish tops
½ stalk celery
1 cup spinach
¼ pear
½ cup pineapple
⅛ cup mixed berries
dash of cayenne
water/ice

Add first 3 ingredients.
Blend until smooth,
adding water as necessary.
Add fruit and blend until
desired consistency.

Look out! This one is spicy! The radish and cayenne work together to prevent ulcers, improve cardiovascular health and clear those clogged nasal passages right up.

The pineapple gives this spicy treat a vibrant tropical flavor and increases energy levels because of its high manganese and thiamin content.

The pear offers just a hint of sweetness and is the perfect amount to keep you from going up in flames.

46. Orange Jewelius

Ingredients

1 handful mixed greens
1 small orange
2 mint leaves
2 basil leaves
½ lemon (juiced)
½ cup young coconut
   meat
water/ice

Blend with water and ice
to desired consistency.

47. Jack Sprout

Ingredients

2–3 Brussels sprouts
(cooked 3–4 minutes)
¼ cup sunflower sprouts
¼ grapefruit (peeled)
½ cup frozen jackfruit
½ lemon (juiced)
½ banana
water

Add first 4 ingredients.
Blend until smooth,
adding water as necessary.
Add fruit and blend until
desired consistency.

Jack is one bitter dude. *This is another one novices should run from. Jack Sprout is bitter, sour and just perfect for the hardcore green-drinker. A vitamin C powerhouse, grapefruit also is a great source of prostate cancer fighting lycopene.*

The Brussels sprouts and sunflower sprouts add tremendous antioxidants and detox power. Jack ain't bitter no more, is he?

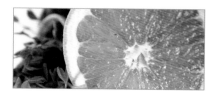

48. Man-Go-Green

Ingredients

1 cup mango
¼ grapefruit
½ kiwi
½ cup collards
2–3 large basil leaves
water/ice

Blend with water and ice
to desired consistency.

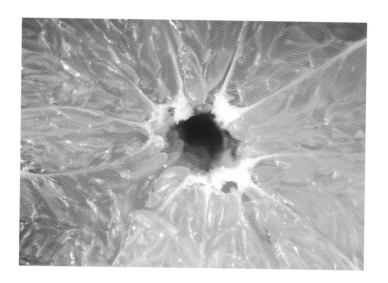

49. American Pie

Ingredients

1 green apple
1 cup spinach
½ cup young coconut
  flesh
½ banana
1 cup coconut water
cinnamon and nutmeg
  to taste

Add first 3 ingredients.
Blend until smooth,
adding water as necessary.
Add fruit and blend until
desired consistency.

Dessert in a glass. *I recommend green-weary kids give this one a go before jumping in to something less sweet. Fresh young coconut is one of the most delicious, healthy fats available. Mixed with sweet apples and protein rich spinach, this is the closest you'll get to eating something akin to Grandma's pie without passing out after eating.*

The banana is not optional in this one, it increases the potassium content of the spinach and adds a creamy pie-like texture that'll have you coming back for more.

50. Superfood Fix

Ingredients

½ cup kale (stemmed)
1 cup spinach
¼ cup blueberry
2 tbsp. frozen acai
2 strawberries
½ cup cantaloupe
1 cup brewed green tea
1 tbsp. flax oil
water/ice

Blend with water and ice
to desired consistency.

51. Lettuce Rock

Ingredients

½ cup lettuce greens
½ cup rocket
½ cup mixed berries
1 small banana
½ lime (juiced)

Add first 2 ingredients.
Blend until smooth,
adding water as necessary.
Add fruit and blend until
desired consistency.

Simplicity. *Sometimes you want nothing to interfere with the music, you know what I'm saying? Lettuce Rock is easy, cost effective to eat everyday, nutritious and delicious.*

The mixed berries (I use frozen as it's even cheaper) add an antioxidant boost while the rocket (arugula) adds a nice bitter flavor that balances well with the sweetness of the banana and the tart of the lime. It's the perfect ensemble. Drink up, rock out.

52. Ginger Drop

Ingredients

1 small bok choy bulb
thumb of peeled ginger
1 small garlic clove
½–1 lemon (juiced)
honey to taste
water/ice

Blend with water and ice
to desired consistency.

Feeling a little under the weather? This drink is great for fighting an oncoming cold.

53. Tom Soy-er

Ingredients

1 Roma tomato
¼ cup Italian parsley
½ stalk celery (soft/white)
1 cup spinach
¼ cup radish tops
Tabasco, black pepper and
    soy sauce to taste
water

Add all ingredients. Blend until smooth, adding water as necessary.

This peppery, salty, spicy tomato tonic will turn you into a modern day warrior with a mean, mean stride. Parsley lends its tumor fighting abilities and also helps increase the antioxidant capacity of the blood.

And if you're a smoker (why would you be?) it also helps neutralize certain types of carcinogens. It's our fresher version of V8 that won't leave you in a sodium coma.

54. Orange Crush

Ingredients

1 large handful spinach
1 orange
1 cup young coconut flesh
water/ice

Blend with water and ice
to desired consistency.

Optional Protein: Hemp
protein powder

55. Blueberry Muffin

Ingredients

1 cup fresh/frozen
    blueberries
2 tbsp. canned pumpkin
1 fig
½ banana
1 small handful baby kale
    leaves
1 tbsp chia seeds
1 cup coconut water

Blend until smooth. Adjust
liquid/ice as necessary.

So many of us like to start our day with something sweet and rich; a doughnut, a bowl of sugary cereal, or a blueberry muffin. Breaking your fast with these sugar-packed sweet pastries makes it very hard to make healthy decisions throughout the rest of your day. Blueberry Muffin is a great compromise. Not only do you get your sweets craving fulfilled with the figs, blueberry, and banana, but you're also doing right by your body.

56. Wild Honey

Ingredients

2 large kale leaves
   (stemmed)
2 large basil leaves
1 cup blackberries
½ banana
1 tbsp. honey
water/ice

Blend with water and ice
to desired consistency.

Optional Protein: Whole
milk plain yogurt

57. Sweet Hot Margarita

Ingredients

1 cup watermelon

½ lemon (juiced)

1 small handful arugula

¼ jalapeno (or to taste)

dash of cayenne

1 tsp. agave nectar (or to taste)

ice

Blend until smooth. Add more water or ice if necessary. Pour into chili-powder-rimmed glass with ice cubes.

This sweet summer shake will heat things up while it cools you down. A spicier take on a morning shake, this drink is the ideal way to kick start your metabolism. Capsaicin found in chili peppers is a powerful agent that helps to boost your metabolic rate and is a known appetite suppressant.

58. Chard Candy

Ingredients

2 chard leaves
1 cup red grapes
2 dates (pitted)
1 tbsp. almond butter
water/ice

Blend with water and ice
to desired consistency.

Optional Protein: Whole,
raw milk

59. Avo-Cooler

Ingredients

1 small bunch watercress
2–4 large mint leaves
½ lime (juiced)
½ cucumber
¼ avocado
water/ice

Blend until smooth. Add ice or water to thin.

This green smoothie is a creamy clean treat. This recipe does double duty for green's lovers and those looking for healthy home skin care solutions. Not only is the avocado a great source of healthy fat, but it is also full of phytonutrients for over-all skin health and complexion.

60. Cocoa Mo

Ingredients

1 kale leaves (stemmed)
1 handful mixed greens
½ apple
½ banana
1 tbsp. almond butter
1–2 tbsp. raw cocao
   powder
vanilla to taste
water/ice

Blend with water and ice
to desired consistency.

Optional Protein: Egg
protein powder

Vanilla extract is fine but try to find some vanilla beans and cut them open, scrape out the insides and use that instead. They're delicious and you rid yourself of the alcohol used in extracts, however little there is.

61. Peach Punch

Ingredients

1 peach (pitted)
1 cup mango
1 bunch lettuce (red leaf
   or mixed)
water/ice

Remove the mango skin
and all pits (stones). Blend
with water or ice.

Optional Protein: Whey
protein powder

The kitchen can be a busy place in the mornings, especially with multiple green drinkers in the house. Rest assured Peach Punch is as simple to prepare as it is to enjoy which makes it perfect for parents and kids alike. A few cups of pre-cut and frozen fruit with a handful of greens is all it takes.

62. Summer Citrus Crush

Ingredients

2 kale leaves (stemmed)
1 cup mango
½ orange
¼ grapefruit
water/ice

Peel the mango, orange, and grapefruit and toss the mango pit. Blend with water and ice to desired consistency.

63. Mangonut Kiwiberry

Ingredients

1–2 large kale leaves
(stemmed)
2–4 strawberries
½ cup mango
½ cup young coconut
meat
½–1 kiwi
water/ice

Remove kiwi and mango skins and pit (stone). Blend and add coconut water/ice as necessary.

Kale is known for it's bold flavor which often deters kids from asking for seconds of this highly nutritious vegetable. However, with Mangonut Kiwiberry kids can really enjoy a bright sweet taste, creamy texture from the coconut, and the healthful benefits that come with drinking their vegetables.

64. Sweet Chard O' Mine

Ingredients

2 chard leaves
1 stalk celery
½ pear
1 cup raspberries
½ lemon (juiced)
water/ice

Blend with water and ice
to desired consistency.

65. Honey Bunch

Ingredients

1 cup honeydew
⅛ avocado
1 handful spinach
⅛ cucumber
water/ice

Blend with water and ice
to desired consistency.

Honey Bunch offers a fresh flavor, and a fresh
face. It can also become an important part of
anyones internal skincare routine. By adding
extra-hydrating foods like honeydew, avocado,
and cucumber to your green drinks you're likely
to see results on the outside as well as in.

66. Banana Rock

Ingredients

1 handful arugula
2 kale leaves (stemmed)
1 tbsp. pumpkin puree
½ pear
½ banana
water/ice

Blend with water and ice
to desired consistency.

Optional Protein: Hemp
protein powder

67. Salsa Fresca

Ingredients

¼ cup cilantro
¼ cup parsley
½ lemon (peeled)
1 apple
ginger to taste
1 small stalk celery
water

Blend with water to desired consistency.

A playful mix of zesty flavor and sweet spice make up this fun drink.

68. Post Marathon

Ingredients

1 Banana (halved)
1 Lemon
1 cup coconut water
water/ice

Blend all ingredients until smooth. Add protein or superfood powder, if necessary, and stir.

One of the most integral parts to post workout recovery is replacing lost fluids, and what better way to do that than with a super food drink? Post Marathon's banana, citrus, and coconut combo meet these needs and are great for electrolyte replenishment. Starting a recovery routine is the best way to enhance overall workout performance and with this drink you are well on your way.

69. Raspberry Pearée

Ingredients

1 small bunch dandelion
  greens
¼ cup fennel
½ pear
½ cup raspberries
½ banana
ginger to taste
water/ice

Blend with water and ice
to desired consistency.

70. Fruit Cocktail

Ingredients

1 cup watermelon
2–3 strawberries
½ cup grapes
2–4 leaves of mint
1 handful mixed greens
water/ice

Blend with ice. Add more watermelon for desired consistency.

71. Coffee Greens

Ingredients

1 large leaf kale
   (stemmed)
1 large leaf chard
   (stemmed)
½ banana
¾ cup macadamia nuts
1 cup brewed coffee
raw cocoa powder to taste
ice

Blend with more brewed
coffee and ice to desired
consistency.

Optional Protein: Whole,
raw milk

72. Plumkin

Ingredients

1 tbsp. pumpkin puree
1 plum (pitted)
1 large handful spinach
1 cup coconut water
cinnamon to taste

Blend and add more
coconut water as
necessary.

Optional Protein: Whole
milk plain yogurt

*Add whole milk, chia seeds or your favorite
protein powder to make the perfect post-
workout recovery green smoothie.*

73. Good Apples

Ingredients

1 small bunch dandelion greens
1 golden apple
1 small banana
water/ice

Blend with water and ice to desired consistency.

74. Tropical Storm

Ingredients

The juice of 2 large carrots
½ cup frozen mango
½ cup frozen pineapple
2 Collard green leaves (stemmed)
5 Basil large leaves
6 Mint leaves
¼ jalapeno

Juice carrots separately. Blend all ingredients together and serve up in a tall glass with a straw.

This great combination provides some fabulous tropical tastes that pack a real healthy punch with a kick of jalapeño. This is sure to get your circulation moving.

Change it up: *Kale and Collard greens are often exchangeable. If you have a preference both options work well with the fruit pairing above.*

75. Col. Mustard Greens

Ingredients

½ cup mustard greens
1 small Roma tomato
⅛ avocado
½ zucchini (cooked)
½ lime (juiced)
favorite herbs to taste

Blend with water to
desired consistency.

Works well with fresh oregano, basil or dill but feel free to experiment with other fresh herbs.

76. Pomapple

Ingredients

1 small handful beet
   greens
1 apple
1 cup pomegranate juice
water/ice

Blend with water and ice
to desired consistency.

77. Proconut

Ingredients

2 kale leaves (stemmed)
⅛ avocado
½ banana
1 cup coconut water
1 tbsp. chia seeds
1 scoop protein powder
  (optional)
water/ice

Blend with water and ice
to desired consistency.

78. Santa Sangria

Ingredients

1 small bunch wild oak
½ cup mango
½ cup red grapes
½ orange
1 small plum (pitted)
1 lime (juiced)
½ cup pomegranate juice
water/ice

Blend with water and ice
to desired consistency.

79. Blind Date 80. Capt. Dr. Kale

Ingredients

1 cup mustard greens
½ cup broccoli sprouts
½ - 1 lemon (juiced)
2 dates (pitted)
½ banana
water/ice

Blend with water and ice
to desired consistency.

Ingredients

1 cup coffee brewed
2 cups of baby kale
1 tbsp cacao nibs
¾ cup almond milk
1 scoop whey protein powder
1 banana
1 large date

Brew up one cup of coffee. Combine coffee
and all ingredients into your NutriBullet and
blend until smooth.

*"Life is short, eat dessert first!" For our
intrepid Capt. Dr. Caela, rounds at the hospital
never stop so its hard to know when dessert
ends and breakfast begins. This shake gives
her all the energy and nutrients she needs to
keep going shift after shift, so she can drink to
your health as well as her own. On the chance
you miss your opportunity for your daily intake
of greens in each meal, there's always dessert.*

81. We Got The Beet

Ingredients

1 small handful beet
  greens
1 cup red grapes
½ apple
½ banana
water/ice

Blend with water and ice
to desired consistency.

82. Shake It Up

Ingredients

1 cup turnip greens
½ cup broccoli sprouts
½ small zucchini (cooked
   3–4 minutes)
½ pear
½ cup young coconut
   meat
1 lime (juiced)
ginger to taste
water/ice

Blend with water and ice
to desired consistency.

83. Chocolate Mint

Ingredients

2 pitted dates
1 cup raw milk
  (or almond milk)
¼ cup soaked almonds
1 tbsp. cacao nibs
½ cup packed mint leaves
½ small avocado
1 cup coconut water

Skin all soaked almonds before placing them and the rest of the ingredients in the NutriBullet to blend to a chunky, minty goodness.

Chocolate and mint together provide a taste treat that never fails to satisfy. Reminiscent of cookie and candy standards Chocolate Mint pays homage to some nostalgic favorites. With this creamy drink you can enjoy the combination guilt free with the added bonus that it is actually good for you!

84. Perfect Post Workout

Ingredients

½ cup cooked organic
   brown rice (cold) or ½
   cup uncooked organic
   rolled oats
2 tbsp. organic raisins
1 scoops of high quality
   protein powder
½ tsp. cinnamon
1 tsp. maca powder
1 cup organic raw whole
   milk
Water

Combine all ingredients
in NutriBullet and blend
until creamy.

After a serious workout where you've depleted your energy stores it's important that you refuel your body to recover and get stronger so that you can meet your next personal record. Combining healthy carbs like rolled oats or organic rice with protein powder and natural sugar from raisins provides the substance you need to avoid muscle depletion and backsliding from your fitness progress.

85. Hello World

Ingredients

½ cup fresh or frozen
   organic blueberries
2 big handfuls of organic
   greens (whatever you
   have on-hand)
½ banana
½ avocado
½ tsp. matcha
1 cup almond ice
1 cup organic raw whole
   milk
Water

Blend with water and ice
to desired consistency.

The perfect introduction to the language of green drinks. A quick look at the source code of this drink and you'll be surprised that its creamy blueberry goodness delivers such great flavor and nutrition. The energy surge will have you coding Hello World every morning.

Compile. *Execute.*

86. Chocolate Protein

Ingredients

1 scoops protein powder
  (chocolate or vanilla)
2 raw organic pastured
  egg yolks
2 tsp. lemon juice
1 tbsp. cacao powder
1 tbsp chia seeds – add
  and stir after blending
Water/Ice

Combine all ingredients
together in NutriBullet and
mix until frothy.

After a satisfying workout it's hard to not just give in and go to the frozen yogurt shop. This post-workout protein powerhouse has everything you need to recover plus such sweet dessert flavors you'll be hitting the gym just so you can run home to blend this baby up and drink it down.

87. Apple Cream

Ingredients

2 handfuls organic spinach
1 organic apple (peeled, cored. and quartered)
½ avocado
2 tsp. spirulina
½ lemon (juice)
½ cup coconut milk
water/ice

Place all ingredients in NutriBullet and blend. Blend until creamy and smooth. Serve with a straw.

Popeye would approve of this flavorful combination of apple, avocado, and spinach as it is also a power booster with the added help of spirulina which contains higher protein levels than red meat. This creamy concoction packs a health punch of flavor!

88. Green Almond

Ingredients

1–2 handfuls organic kale
1 small banana
1 tbsp. almond butter
2 cups almond ice
water

Blend together all
ingredients with your
NutriBullet until creamy.
Serve immediately.

This drink is loaded with nutrients and is a real palate pleaser. The combination of sweet bananas and almond flavor blend with the kale to make a fresh superfood smoothie.

89. Blue Chai Crunch

Ingredients

1 cup fresh or frozen
organic blueberries

½ cup acai berries (frozen)
or 1 tbsp. powder

1 tbsp. chai tea (powder)

1 ½ tbsp. chia seeds

1 tsp. vanilla extract

2 cups organic raw whole
milk or almond milk

1 tbsp. dried mulberries
on top

Add all ingredients except
dried mulberries to
NutriBullet and blend until
smooth. Top with dried
mulberries.

The wonderful crunchy texture of the dried
mulberry topping on this smoothie adds rustic
appeal as well as flavor. The ingredients like
acai berries compound the flavors as well as the
benefits of disease fighting antioxidants. This
delectable drink will be enjoyed in all its chewy
goodness.

90. Soup To Goji

Ingredients

2 organic roma tomatoes
1 handful organic parsley
1 handful organic cilantro
⅓ organic cucumber
   (peeled)
1 clove garlic
1–2 tbsp. goji berries
½ cup lemon (juice)
½ cup water
1 tbsp extra virgin olive
   oil
salt, pepper, and cayenne
   to taste

Our play on a savory summer soup favorite, Soup To Goji adds a sour spicy element to the rustic italian flavors of a classic gazpatcho. Goji berries are great additions to many savory snacks.

Place all ingredients, save for the oil, into your NutriBullet. After initially blended, drizzle the oil in slowly. Serve in bowl or large cappuccino mug with a spoon.

91. Blue Hippie

Ingredients

2 cups fresh or frozen
   organic blueberries
1 tbsp. chia seeds (powder)
1 tbsp. flaxseed (powder)
1 tbsp. hemp seed
   (powder)
1 tbsp. coconut oil
2 cups almond milk

Place all ingredients into
NutriBullet and blend
until smooth.

*Far out, man! Get the intense health boost
of antioxidants in blueberries with the added
benefits of hemp and flax seeds made creamy
with almond milk. This drink will definitely make
you one with the earthy flavors and feel totally
groovy.*

92. Post Marathon 2

Ingredients

½ cup soaked almonds
½ cup coconut milk
½ cup coconut water
2 tbsp. cacao nibs
1 vanilla bean or 1 tsp
    extract
1–2 tsp. pure maple syrup
    (optional)
½ tsp. sea salt
ice

Skip the cookie sheet! Skin almonds and place in NutriBullet with all other delicious ingredients. Blend until it resembles chocolate chip ice cream. Serve with a straw and enjoy the cacao crunch!

You could say I have a bit of a cookie problem. It's sometimes difficult balancing good taste with a good diet. Our at home Paleo Chocolate Cookie recipe inspired this next drink and had surprisingly positive results. Sweet and savory combinations with the added plus of incorporating superfoods giving you cookies-in-milk all at once without the unfortunate dilemma.

93. Breakfast Smoothie

Ingredients

1 frozen banana
½ cup organic rolled oats
1 tbsp. hemp seeds
1 tsp. maqui berry powder
water/ice
cinnamon and sea salt to
    taste

Blend all together in
NutriBullet. Dust with
cinnamon and serve.

Quality time for breakfast most mornings is non-existent. This smoothie is something good you can do for yourself that won't take time but will send you out into the world fortified with a tasty drink that will stick to your ribs.

94. Creamy Walnut

Ingredients

1 tbsp. flaxseed

¼ cup soaked walnuts

2 dates (pitted)

½ cup organic whole milk yogurt

½ cup fresh young coconut water

ice

stevia to taste (optional)

Blend all ingredients together and enjoy!

The rich natural flavor of walnuts combined with dates and yogurt bring out the nutty goodness of this drink. Flaxseed delivers a fiber boost that is healthy and satisfying any time of the day.

95. Autumn Boost

Ingredients

½ cup organic
    unsweetened pumpkin
    puree
½ overripe pear
2 tbsp. acai powder
2 tbsp. flaxseed
2 tbsp. dried mulberries
1 cup coconut water
ice

Blend all ingredients
(except mulberries)
together, sprinkle with
mulberries, serve with
a straw.

Rich pumpkin promotes healthy skin and high fiber combined with acai age defying benefits makes this team a pretty tasty pair. This harvest time multi-superfood concoction is like pumpkin pie for your skin!

96. Blood Orange Julius

Ingredients

1 blood orange (peeled)
¾ cup organic whole milk
  yogurt
½ cup dried mulberries
1 vanilla bean or ½ tsp
  extract
1 tsp. honey
½ cup coconut water
ice

Juice blood orange and
set aside (if you have a
juicer). Blend all other
ingredients together.
Once blended, mix in the
orange juice and blend
some more.

*Pretty in pink, this creamy dreamsicle smoothie
will absolutely surprise you. Its sinful flavor
conceals its healthful nature. With every sip
you'd never guess you were intaking healthy
probiotics, fighting disease, and reducing
inflammation.*

97. Chocolate Chai

Ingredients

2 tbsp. flaxseed
1 cup chai tea
½ cup organic raw whole
    milk
1 frozen banana
2 tbsp. cacao nibs
ice

Blend all ingredients
together in your NutriBullet.

Give in to the wonderful flavors of chocolate and banana melding together with a creamy chai tea. Even more enjoyable when you know they are packing potassium and antioxidants in the same glass.

98. Orange Liquorice

Ingredients

3 blood oranges
2 kale leaves
1 small fennel bulb
1½ thumb of ginger
1 cup mineral water

Combine all ingredients together in NutriBullet and mix until frothy.

Our superfood Orange Liquorice is an artisanal approach to superfood drinks. Spicy ginger, sweet blood oranges, and kale that gives you a zingy lift while promoting heart health.

99. Vitamin Seaweed

Ingredients

1 pink grapefruit (peeled)
2 cups pineapple fresh/
   frozen
1 orange (peeled)
2 tsp. spirulina
1 handful spinach

Combine all ingredients together in your NutriBullet and mix until frothy.

Changing your diet isn't easy, and often times it's hard to remember not to "drink your calories". Vitamin Seaweed makes this problem so much easier. A natural hunger-buster, pink grapefruit is also said to help boost your metabolism. Getting the proper amount of protein is also important with any diet and spirulina is a great source of protein and nutrients. This drink is also really great for vegetarians and pregnant mothers looking to add protein to their diets.

100. Carrot Spice

Ingredients

1 cup carrot juice
¼ fennel bulb
¾ cup organic raw whole milk
¼ tsp nutmeg
1 vanilla bean or ½ tsp. extract

Combine all ingredients together in your NutriBullet and mix until frothy.

If you are having a hard time choosing between your orange juice in the morning, let us help you make it easier. Carrot Spice takes a sophisticated stand as "the other" orange morning drink. Just like oranges, carrots contain high levels of vitamin C, but have many other properties attributed to cancer fighting and detoxing.

Adding grass-fed whole milk and fennel not only adds digestive health and reduces inflammation to the list of benefits, but creates an earthy and creamy sweetness that makes it an easy choice for your go to "orange" juice.

101. Maca Milk

Ingredients

1 cup almond milk
1 tsp. maca powder
   (dependent)
¼ tsp cinnamon
1 cup water
1 vanilla bean or 1 tsp.
   extract

Combine all ingredients
together in your NutriBullet
and mix until frothy.

Maca root is gaining popularity in the health community as being a superfood that delivers so many positive benefits in just the smallest amount. Besides being beneficial to the circulatory system it's also said to improve brain function and memory, and reduce anxiety. This supplement should not be taken everyday and the dose should be gradually increased starting at ½ tsp per serving.